EXPLORING THE
CHESAPEAKE BAY

T0022555

SAVING
THE CHESAPEAKE BAY

By Ryan Nagelhout

Gareth Stevens
Publishing

Please visit our website, www.garethstevens.com. For a free color catalog of all our high-quality books, call toll free 1-800-542-2595 or fax 1-877-542-2596.

Library of Congress Cataloging-in-Publication Data

Nagelhout, Ryan.
Saving the Chesapeake Bay / by Ryan Nagelhout.
   p. cm. — (Exploring the Chesapeake Bay)
Includes index.
ISBN 978-1-4339-9785-3 (pbk.)
ISBN 978-1-4339-9786-0 (6-pack)
ISBN 978-1-4339-9784-6 (library binding)
1. Chesapeake Bay (Md. and Va.)—Juvenile literature. 2. Wildlife conservation—Chesapeake Bay (Md. and Va.) I. Nagelhout, Ryan. II. Title.
F187.C5 N34 2014
975.2—d23

First Edition

Published in 2014 by
Gareth Stevens Publishing
111 East 14th Street, Suite 349
New York, NY 10003

Copyright © 2014 Gareth Stevens Publishing

Designer: Andrea Davison-Bartolotta
Editor: Kristen Rajczak

Photo credits: Cover, pp. 1, 22, 23 Mary F. Calvert/MCT via Getty Images; p. 5 courtesy of the USDA; p. 7 SSPL/Getty Images; pp. 8, 29 Lone Wolf Photos/Shutterstock.com; p. 9 Cameron Davidson/Stone/Getty Images; p. 10 (John Smith) Kean Collection/Getty Images; pp. 10 (map), 16 Wikimedia Commons; p. 11 Peter Essick/Aurora/Getty Images; p. 12 Jack Dermid/Photo Researchers/Getty Images; pp. 13, 17 (main) Emory Kristof/National Geographic/Getty Images; p. 14 Glowimages/Getty Images; p. 15 Comstock/Thinkstock; p. 17 (inset) Sarah L. Voisin/The Washington Post via Getty Images; pp. 18, 19 (main), 20, 21, 25, 28 Mary Hollinger/NOAA; p. 19 (inset) Gary Meszaros/Visuals Unlimited/Getty Images; p. 24 Scott Neville/The Washington Post via Getty Images; p. 26 (all) iStockphoto/Thinkstock; p. 27 Globe Turner/Shutterstock.com.

Printed in the United States of America

CPSIA compliance information: Batch #CS13GS: For further information contact Gareth Stevens, New York, New York at 1-800-542-2595.

CONTENTS

Words in the glossary appear in **bold** type the first time they are used in the text.

AN ESSENTIAL ESTUARY

The Chesapeake Bay is the largest **estuary** in the United States. It brings the Atlantic Ocean inland, where salt water meets and mixes with the freshwater of 150 rivers and streams that flow into the bay. Over the years, major changes to the region have harmed the health of the bay and its plants and wildlife.

Once lush with greenery, clear water, and lots of animals, the Chesapeake Bay is an **ecosystem** in danger. Poor waste treatment, expanding towns, and overfishing have ruined wetlands, destroyed plant life, and hurt animal populations. America's essential estuary is in danger, but it can be saved.

THE WATERSHED

A watershed is an area of land whose water drains into a particular river or waterway. The Chesapeake Bay's watershed covers about 64,000 square miles (165,760 sq km). It occupies parts of six states—Delaware, Maryland, New York, Pennsylvania, Virginia, and West Virginia—as well as all of Washington, DC. What happens here, even hundreds of miles away, can have a big impact on the bay's health.

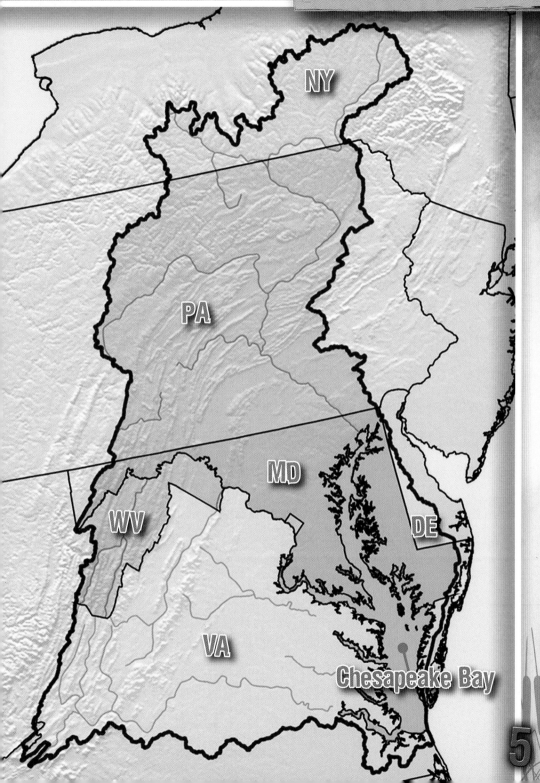

NY

PA

MD

WV

DE

VA

Chesapeake Bay

ABOUT THE BAY

The Chesapeake Bay formed nearly 12,000 years ago when glaciers melted and flooded the Susquehanna River valley to form a **ria**. Historians think the bay's name comes from the Algonquian word *chesepiooc*.

The Chesapeake Bay has 3,830 square miles (9,920 sq km) of surface area, of which a small part is tidal freshwater or salt water. But about 3,560 square miles (9,220 sq km) is brackish water, or areas where freshwater and salt water mix. The fascinating ecosystem also has more than 1,500 square miles (3,885 sq km) of wetlands, which serve as a **habitat** for fish, shellfish, and other wildlife.

THE TRIBUTARIES

Five major river systems supply the Chesapeake Bay with its freshwater. The Potomac, the Susquehanna, the Rappahannock, the York, and the James Rivers all drain into the Chesapeake Bay, along with dozens of smaller rivers and streams. The health of those rivers is very important to the overall health of the bay. Over 85,800 cubic feet (2,400 cu m) of freshwater flow into the Chesapeake Bay per second!

Glaciers are big sheets of ice. At one time, they covered much of the bay watershed, carving some of the waterways.

BAY BIOMES

Many different plants and animals call the Chesapeake Bay's various **biomes** home. The watershed's coastline is longer than the entire West Coast of the United States, offering many different habitats for creatures and vegetation.

The Chesapeake Bay supports **riparian** hardwood forests, shallow water areas filled with underwater grasses, open water with fish and shellfish, and inlets and islands teeming with waterfowl. The bay's freshwater tributaries have important biomes that—though often hundreds of miles away—can affect the bay. With so many plants and animals living in the watershed's varied habitats, protecting the health of the Chesapeake Bay is a complicated task.

GREAT BLUE HERON

The Chesapeake Bay has an average depth of just 21 feet (6.4 m) and drops to 174 feet (53 m) at its deepest point near Annapolis, Maryland. It supports more than 3,600 species, or kinds, of plant and animal life, including 2,700 types of plants and at least 16 species of underwater grasses. Its waters hold 348 species of fish and 173 kinds of shellfish.

Riparian forests protect shorelines and filter ground and surface water.

PEOPLE AND THE BAY

People have lived around the Chesapeake Bay for thousands of years, but major problems arrived with European settlers in the 1600s. Settlers used wide bands of farmland for tobacco growth and cut down ancient trees. Their actions upset the natural balance of habitats and began harming the area.

With bountiful fish and wildlife and good land for crops, people flooded into the Chesapeake Bay to make a living off its natural resources. At first, very little was done to **conserve** its resources. By the middle of the 18th century, **deforestation** had sent large amounts of dirt into the bay. Colonists noticed the Chesapeake Bay looked cloudier.

MAP OF THE CHESAPEAKE BAY FROM THE EARLY 1600S

Forests once covered almost 95 percent of the Chesapeake Bay watershed. They were often cleared for farmland.

JOHN SMITH'S CHESAPEAKE

In 1608, Captain John Smith, an English explorer governing at Jamestown, Virginia, set out to explore the Chesapeake Bay. He mapped the area and noted its beauty, writing "heaven and Earth have never agreed better to frame a place for man's habitation." Smith's descriptions of plant and animal life tell scientists and historians what the Chesapeake Bay looked like before settlement changed conditions in the watershed.

While building towns and cities, most settlers had little understanding of how much they could damage the **environment**. Fishing became big business in the Chesapeake Bay, and despite some laws prohibiting hunting and **dredging**, animal populations fell dramatically. Overfishing has been a major problem for centuries. Commercial fishing put many species at risk, and fish **hatcheries** were opened as early as the 1870s.

Beds of oysters, which John Smith said once "lay as thick as stones," were ripped up. By 1885, 20 million bushels of oysters were harvested per year. Eventually, fisherman started coming back with smaller hauls.

OYSTER REEFS IN A CREEK

WHITE GOLD

Oyster harvesting once made up much of the fishing market in the Chesapeake Bay. Fishermen used to call it "white gold" and fought over catches. Production increased when boats called skipjacks were made to navigate the bay's shallows. New canning techniques and advances in refrigeration helped ship oysters all over the country. Oyster populations decreased. By 1993, only 80,000 bushels were being harvested per year.

In recent decades, disease has also contributed to decreasing oyster populations.

THE HUMAN TOUCH

Lots of industrial waste was dumped into the Chesapeake Bay during the 19th and 20th centuries. Pollution from factories built during the 1800s turned the sky black with smoke. But today, perhaps the greatest threat to the bay is population growth.

In the 1850s, the bay's population was around 2 million people. Now, the Chesapeake Bay is home to more than 17 million people—10 million alone on the coastline—with about 100,000 people moving into the watershed each year.

All these people need land for homes and highways to get to work. They create tons of waste each year.

BALTIMORE SEWAGE TREATMENT PLANT

BATTLEGROUND BALTIMORE

Baltimore, Maryland, is a major cause of pollution for the Chesapeake Bay. The city's aging sewage treatment system often leaks raw waste into waterways after heavy rains, and old pipes leak and harm waterways. The city's officials have said $2 billion will be spent to overhaul about 3,100 miles (4,990 km) of its waste system, but many worry it won't be enough to stop the overwhelming pollution the city creates.

More people and bigger cities and suburbs mean more pollution going into the watershed. The graph below shows the growing population.

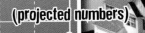
(projected numbers)

millions of people

24

18

12

6

0

1950 1960 1970 1980 1990 2000 2010 2020 2030

year

HABITAT HAVOC

When estuaries aren't healthy, animal populations suffer. Many **endangered** species call the Chesapeake Bay home, including shortnose sturgeon and green sea turtles. These animals are protected from harm by laws, and their populations are monitored closely.

Other commercial fishing targets are in serious jeopardy as well. Eastern oyster populations have been described as "commercially extinct" in the Chesapeake Bay. Pollution, overfishing, and dams that block access to spawning grounds have hurt shad, once the most profitable finfish in the Chesapeake Bay. Striped bass saw serious population declines in the 1970s and 1980s, while blue crabs have lost much of their habitat due to poor water quality.

SHORTNOSE
STURGEON

MENHADEN MADNESS

People don't eat one of the most important fish in the Chesapeake Bay. Menhaden, tiny fish that swim in schools, are an important food source for bluefish, weakfish, and striped bass as well as some birds like osprey. However, millions are caught each year to make fish oils and other products. One company based in Reedville, Virginia, owns more than 80 percent of the menhaden fished in the world!

With laws limiting some commercial fishing, skipjacks like this one may be docked for a long time.

PLANT PERIL

Thousands of plants play an essential part in keeping the Chesapeake Bay stable. Pollution and other factors can also impact their presence in the estuary.

Submerged aquatic vegetation, or SAV, is incredibly important to water quality in the Chesapeake Bay. These grasses and plants provide underwater creatures with food and habitats, filter the water, prevent loss of soil, and supply oxygen to the water. Pollution and extreme weather hurt SAV growth in the Chesapeake Bay, which makes it a good measure of overall bay health.

In addition, between 1982 and 1997, the bay watershed lost more than 750,000 acres (304,000 ha) of forestland—about 100 acres (41 ha) per day.

Erosion, or the movement of soil by wind and water, caused these trees to fall into the marsh.

INVASIVE SPECIES

Some plants and animals not native to the Chesapeake Bay have hurt its health. There are more than 150 of these invasive species, some of which have taken habitats, food supplies, and other resources from animals and plants native to the bay. Among the invasive species, mute swans, nutria, phragmites, purple loosestrife, water chestnuts, and zebra mussels are considered the worst.

ZEBRA MUSSELS

SAV is harmed by poor water quality because it needs light to grow.

FIXING THE BAY

Occasional efforts were made by local governments to help animal populations in early America. Seasons were established for hunting, and some states outlawed commercial hunting and dredging, but they did little to prevent pollution.

It wasn't until the 1970s that interest was drawn to true conservation. In 1972, Hurricane Agnes destroyed wetlands and brought a lot of soil and pollution into the bay. That same year, the federal government passed the Clean Water Act, which made water quality standards the same for every state. The Environmental Protection Agency, or EPA, began to focus on the Chesapeake Bay.

Many scientists and conservation groups began studying the Chesapeake Bay during the 1970s. The US Army Corps of Engineers assessed bay conditions in 1973 and predicted what it would be like in 2020. The results shocked scientists and bay residents, who began to realize action needed to be taken. More groups formed and put pressure on the government to protect the estuary.

By taking water samples from the Chesapeake Bay, scientists and conservation groups can learn about what's in the bay's water and causing harm.

FIGHTING BACK

People are accountable for much of the immense harm done to the Chesapeake Bay over the years, but they have also worked hard to preserve and revive it. In 1983, government officials in the bay watershed signed the Chesapeake Bay Agreement. They pledged to restore and protect bay waters and wildlife, as well as manage industries affecting them.

Another Chesapeake Bay Agreement was signed in 1987, establishing specific goals led by the newly formed Chesapeake Bay Program. The program unites many efforts of various government agencies, nonprofit organizations, and academic partners in an estuary that reaches over 18,000 local governments.

Since then, enormous conservation projects have taken place in the Chesapeake Bay's watershed.

TEST PLOT #1	TEST PLOT #2	TEST PLOT #3	TEST PLOT #4
Two feet of unconsolidated dredged material placed with excavation equipment.	Two feet of consolidated dredged material tilled with farming equipment.	Two feet of tilled dredged material covered with six inches of sand.	Two feet of tilled dredged material covered with twelve inches of sand.

REPORT CARD

Since 1991, the Chesapeake Bay Foundation has released State of the Bay reports that review the health of the Chesapeake Bay. The report now uses 13 different markers such as water clarity, dissolved oxygen levels, and animal population to score the Chesapeake Bay's overall health. The scale runs from 1 to 100, with a score of 70 representing a "saved" bay.

A muskrat feeds in marsh grass that was hand planted as part of a restoration project at Poplar Island near Talbot County, Maryland.

CHANGING WEATHER

Rising global temperatures have had a big impact on the Chesapeake Bay. Changing weather cycles create big storms like hurricanes, which can wash pollution into the bay and upset plant and animal habitats. The balance between freshwater, salt water, and brackish water can shift quickly with changing weather patterns. Efforts to slow changes in climate can help preserve the Chesapeake Bay's conditions and prevent rising water levels.

Restoration efforts in the Chesapeake Bay have targeted improving bay grasses, restoring wetlands and oyster reefs, and reopening fish passages. Scientists carefully study the bay's wildlife.

In 2010, the EPA established a "pollution diet" to limit wastes and clean up the bay's water. Other efforts to restore forests and protect land have improved the health of the watershed. Industrial and human waste is also closely monitored.

Meanwhile, "weed warriors" are trained to remove invasive plant species. Today, scientists are making plans to remove invasive animals. They encourage the use of "green" energy and building options within the watershed to protect the environment.

These divers are planting wild celery in the bay with a group from the Cheasapeake Bay Foundation.

MAPPING THE BAY'S HEALTH

Each year, the Chesapeake Bay's health is rated. This map shows the grades each area of the bay watershed earned in 2011. How do they figure out the bay's grades? Check out the factors that are measured and considered during grading below.

Bay Health Indicators:

 Water clarity, or the amount of light that can get through the water

 Chlorophyll *a*, a measurement of phytoplankton biomass, or the living and dead matter in the water

State of aquatic grasses

 Amount of dissolved oxygen

 Benthic Index of Biotic Integrity, or a measure of the conditions of the creatures living in or on the bottom of the bay

 Phytoplankton Index of Biotic Integrity, or a measure of algae conditions

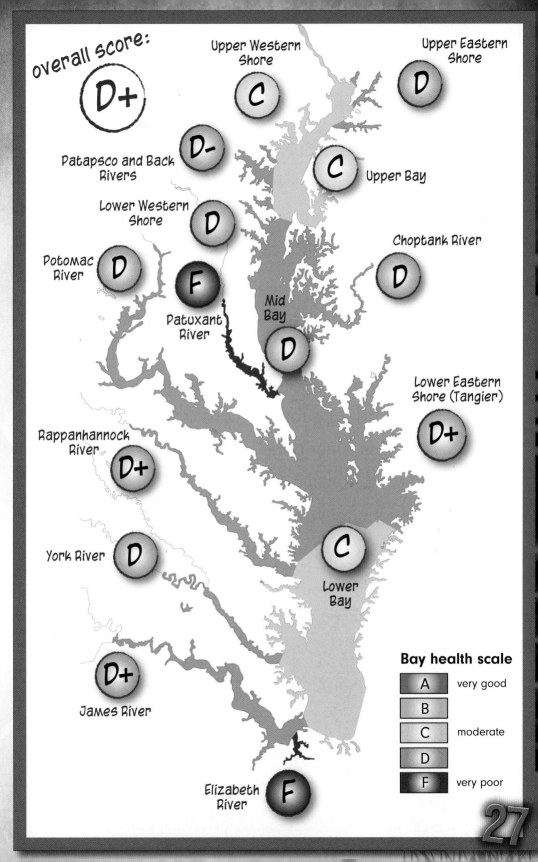

overall score:

D+

Upper Western Shore

C

Upper Eastern Shore

D

Patapsco and Back Rivers

D-

Upper Bay

C

Lower Western Shore

D

Choptank River

D

Potomac River

D

Patuxent River

F

Mid Bay

D

Lower Eastern Shore (Tangier)

D+

Rappanhannock River

D+

York River

D

Lower Bay

C

James River

D+

Elizabeth River

F

Bay health scale

A	very good
B	
C	moderate
D	
F	very poor

SLOW PROGRESS

Recovery is measurable but slow. The 2012 State of the Bay report gave the bay an overall rating of 32. It's far from the 70 representing a "saved" bay and even further from the 100 of the unharmed bay John Smith once observed.

Eastern oyster populations remain low, and the threat of climate change is ever present, but a concerted effort is being made to save the Chesapeake Bay. Groups are constantly working to raise awareness among the millions of people living in the watershed, asking them to limit pollution and pressure government agencies to act.

However, saving the Chesapeake Bay remains a work in progress.

PATUXENT RIVER

YOU CAN HELP!

If you live within the watershed, encourage your parents to grow plants without using chemicals and collect downspout water into a rain barrel to water plants. You can join conservation groups or write letters to people in your government and tell them to help protect the bay! Maybe someday you'll be one of the scientists studying the Chesapeake Bay.

Despite troubling environmental conditions, many parts of the Chesapeake Bay are beautiful.

GLOSSARY

biome: a large community of plants and animals living in the same conditions

conserve: to keep safe and avoid waste

deforestation: the clearing of wide areas of trees

dredge: to scoop or suck up something under shallow water

ecosystem: all the living things in an area

endangered: at risk of dying out, or going extinct

environment: the natural world in which a plant or animal lives

estuary: a place where freshwater and salt water bodies meet

habitat: the place where an animal lives

hatchery: a place where fish eggs are hatched, and fish are artificially controlled

ria: a coastal inlet formed by flooding a river valley

riparian: living on the bank of a waterway

FOR MORE INFORMATION

Books

Bennett, Kelly. *Chesapeake Bay*. New York, NY: Children's Press, 2006.

Langley, Andrew. *Saving the Environment*. Chicago, IL: Heinemann Library, 2013.

Marsico, Katie. *The Chesapeake Bay*. Ann Arbor, MI: Cherry Lake Publishing, 2013.

Websites

Chesapeake Bay Program: How To's and Tips
chesapeakebay.net/takeaction/howtotips
Learn how you can help conservation efforts in the Chesapeake Bay.

Chesapeake Bay Foundation
cbf.org
Read reports and find out what you can do to help save the Chesapeake Bay.

ChesapeakeStat
stat.chesapeakebay.net
Make your own map of data collected by scientists studying the Chesapeake Bay!

INDEX